HOMEWORK AND HEARTSTRINGS

HOMEWORK AND HEARTSTRINGS

Supporting Your Child's Learning Alone

AVERY NIGHTINGALE

Creative Quill Press

CONTENTS

1	Introduction	1
2	Understanding the Importance of Homework	3
3	Creating a Supportive Environment	5
4	Establishing a Homework Routine	7
5	Providing Encouragement and Motivation	9
6	Setting Realistic Expectations	11
7	Helping with Time Management	13
8	Teaching Effective Study Skills	15
9	Assisting with Homework Assignments	17
10	Addressing Challenges and Frustrations	19
11	Promoting Independence and Responsibility	20
12	Utilizing Technology as a Learning Tool	22
13	Balancing Homework with Other Activities	24
14	Communicating with Teachers and School Staff	26
15	Recognizing and Celebrating Achievements	27
16	Supporting Emotional Well-being	29
17	Encouraging Critical Thinking and Problem-Solving	31

18	Providing Resources for Additional Help	33
19	Monitoring Progress and Tracking Improvement	35
20	Facilitating Peer Collaboration and Support	37
21	Promoting a Growth Mindset	39
22	Fostering a Love for Learning	41
23	Encouraging Effective Note-Taking	43
24	Teaching Organization and Time Management Skills	45
25	Addressing Procrastination and Time Wasting Habits	47
26	Helping with Test Preparation and Exam Strategies	49
27	Supporting Reading Comprehension and Writing Skills	51
28	Promoting Healthy Sleep Habits	53
29	Encouraging Physical Activity and Breaks	55
30	Nurturing Creativity and Critical Thinking	57
31	Balancing Screen Time and Homework	59
32	Conclusion	61

Copyright © 2024 by Avery Nightingale

All rights reserved. No part of this book may be reproduced in any manner whatsoever without written permission except in the case of brief quotations embodied in critical articles and reviews.

First Printing, 2024

CHAPTER 1

Introduction

So I want to provide a resource not just for teaching specific content, but for the whole process of guiding at-home learning. I want to show you how valuable everyday life is as part of your child's education. And, because it is such a large part of both your child's daily schedule and your heart, this document has more than one part about homework. However, I will try to keep defining my terms as I go so you can quickly skip ahead (not be held hostage to however much I can write) if the one thing you need help with today is your first- or second-grader's homework. I hope you notice and appreciate my strategy of repeating myself frequently – one, to help you remember the ideas that will help you strengthen your child's education, and two, to realize that any set of resources from school will do essentially the same thing. So you don't have to be afraid to experiment, add, or completely disregard any of my suggestions as you see which ones make a real difference in learning in your home.

Thank you for caring enough to read this. My heart goes out to those adults who are carrying the entire burden of their children's learning while we have our schools closed. As an educator, I know that many of you are overwhelmed by your multiple responsibilities, possibly homeschooling several children in several grades at once. I hope this document can help a bit. (Full disclosure: I have no children myself and I do not envy you right now!!) As I hear from schoolteacher friends about how they are reaching out to support their families right now, I realize that I mostly can't just "send home the next packet and cheerfully talk to you and your child every some days during distance learning." You have most of the responsibility for presenting new concepts and guiding your child's at-home learning. Each of you is in a unique and complex situation.

CHAPTER 2

Understanding the Importance of Homework

- Children approach homework with an attitude ranging from "I'm just not getting this!" to "Why are they making me study all of this on my time? They're the ones being paid to teach us at school." This kind of thinking has been around practically from the beginning of the public school system, but these days, in particular, it's even becoming something kids voice to their parents. - Learning at home before the school's content has been learned always produces positive learning results. "What about memorizing vocabulary first in order to not only increase test scores but also score higher when practicing conversation?" - Parents always want to help with the problems of their children's "private lives", but when looking at homework, they always consider it a "private place of learning exclusively for the student". If you give it more thought however, if your daughter or son was in any sort of trouble where a 3-person team could solve it even more quickly, wouldn't it be to the great satisfaction of all three people? No? Is that something that should be left only to two of the three? Let's think more on this...

The matter of homework is usually misunderstood by both parents and the children themselves, causing the following to happen:

A school principal once told parents that if they became more involved in their children's homework, the students' level of "home learning" would increase. When experimenting with the help, encouragement, and guidance of their parents, even kids using trial-and-error problem-solving strategies could do better than children stuck in a frustrating time loop, all bundled up in the chaos of their own minds. Success always raised their energy level, which drowned out the discouraging self-criticism of any mistakes leading to improvement.

CHAPTER 3

Creating a Supportive Environment

Though I can almost always guarantee that a student who has both time and resources will improve their education, we cannot guarantee that every family will have those resources. But we can guarantee that every student has a family, however that family may be defined, and every family has happiness and time to spend to ensure the success of the student in their midst. The practice of education in this world can then become not just one of dictating rules and curriculum, but a practice of what is truly important in life: supporting each other. With that, adhuc omnia pueri agunt (as the boys are busy still) and ever learning, the practice of family endeavors to allow that the rest of their concerns have spring. There is a lesson in that that goes beyond even Latin homework.

Licatha observes that "the students attend with their tutoring money already in hand, paying before each lesson on their own initiative without ever being prompted, some of them even working to earn their tutoring fee, or more, before our lesson together. Their parents and teachers also put in an enormous amount of work to make it all happen." Notice how much the responsibility lies with the student, and how much support comes from the parents and teachers. This work ethic and approachability is very commonly shared between successful students and their families. Very seldom was a devoted student just that. These devoted students just as often relied on and in turn valued the devoted teachers and parents around them. For such devoted students, hard work for their own education is not a hassle or a problem but a privilege and a question of who did the most work.

CHAPTER 4

Establishing a Homework Routine

Once you have a homework time established, your child will also expect your availability at that time. By age six or seven, most children are accustomed to falling into a routine; their bodies are programmed to naturally expect things like lunch and bedtime at certain times. If they can also depend on you to be available for homework help during a specific time of day, they will learn to prepare for it and be more cooperative. After that established time, stop providing direct assistance and begin helping from a distance. "Assistance" can range from direct help (showing your child how to overhand serve a volleyball) to sharing nearby support (offering to take your child to volleyball practice). Don't forget to draw the line to ensure that the child's work is her own, though, such as telling the child that you can't serve the ball, as you don't know how to play volleyball—standing by and providing encouragement empowers the child to think for herself.

Schedule the homework session for a specific time before or after your child has some time to unwind at home—such as after an after-school snack or an hour of playing outside. If your work schedule does not allow consistency in the exact time, at least start the homework as soon as the child is home from school or as soon as the family finishes their evening meal. Choose a time and place where you can give the child your undivided attention. If you have more than one child, supervise the homework time in different parts of the house or at different times and help a child known for procrastinating first, so that he or she has less time to get off track.

CHAPTER 5

Providing Encouragement and Motivation

Remember that all behavior is based on motivation. Struggle in academic areas, like many types of learning, can be painful, so try to make it a pleasant, non-painful experience as much as possible. The way to do this is to be encouragement focused. I believe that feedback should help children see themselves accurately, value themselves, and then begin to show the same appreciation for their efforts that we do. So, when talking with your children about performance areas, focus equally on strengths and room for growth, being as specific as possible. The review should include expression and acknowledgment of your trust and anticipation that, if your child can trust that your feedback is always developmentally honest, they will come to trust your encouragement and motivation for adjusting and refining future effort. Make sure the review also includes a strategic collaboration on what needs to change, or can stay the same, and for what reasons.

Take the time to recognize effort and offer words of encouragement no matter what your child's age is. If your children are young, you might offer verbal praise or a special privilege. As they get older, you may offer less praise and more respect or validation of their efforts. For example, if your young child reads a difficult book, you might tell them, "I'm really proud of the way you kept working on that book, even when it was hard," and offer extra time snuggled in a rocking chair together. For an older child who has done well on a project or test they worked hard to prepare for, you might say with genuine astonishment and respect, "You must be very proud of the way that you honored your work with that quality, that it went so well for you. It was worth all that energy and dedication, wasn't it?"

CHAPTER 6

Setting Realistic Expectations

Setting realistic expectations for the amount of parental involvement and time available for helping your child with homework can be invaluable to your peace of mind. In a recent policy statement, the NRC urged teachers to set realistic homework expectations given the reality of the families they are serving. But how do you know what is realistic? You probably have more of a sense of how much time you can conceivably devote to homework help than most teachers and probably more importantly you are keenly aware of other priorities—yours, your child's, and other family obligations—that homework help must compete with. You can aid in the upholding of the NRC's advice by openly and calmly talking with your child's teacher and other parents about your and their homework help experiences. A spirited discussion about the importance of setting realistic expectations for homework help can be the underpinning of permission to provide the necessary support from home.

It's 9:15 PM, that is! You just finished the last of the dinner dishes and a 45-minute bedtime routine. You sit down finally, thinking about the book of essays that's due for book group on Wednesday and wondering when you can find the time. Then you remember. Homework! The letters on the informational flyer you saw sitting on the couch earlier tonight pop into your head. Would you remember the homework assignment that your child was unable to finish, to go over, to understand at all? To help with. They never stop. So when you remember, you want to help, but all you really want to know is when can you go to bed?

CHAPTER 7

Helping with Time Management

This section is the next in the series of strategies on how to help children who are not learning with adults after school. Other sections have already been or are being planned to be written about increasing intrinsic motivation, learning from textbooks, recognizing and filling in gaps, deciding when and what to memorize, learning from homework, and writing essays. Between the two parts, I am going to insert a caution about not helping too much, and you might find it interesting how adults learn alone to get insights about your children's or students' learning style.

What would your children do if you weren't there to keep them on track for homework and learn alone (HAL) after school? My son J. gets home long before I do, and I practically never gave him directions or told him to hurry up. He does his homework on his own before I get home. I was curious about how he did it, so once I asked him. His answer was – "Ummm, I don't know. I mean, I do, but I really don't know." That evening, when he finished his homework, I asked him to think back and try to remember what had worked, and we categorized it into 3 principles: Focus, Discipline, and Strategy. Then we elaborated on what he specifically had done for reading and math. There are seven "big picture" strategies which you can teach your kids to help them manage time.

CHAPTER 8

Teaching Effective Study Skills

Long story short, all too often, many children don't have a natural driving passion for understanding the world of science that surrounds them. This is a tough truth to face when kids are climbing all over you asking you to buy things that look incredibly exciting to them. What happens when learning for learning's sake is fun, but what is being handed out by the school doesn't feel fun? What happens when things start to feel "operatesque"? Therein lies the challenge. Everything feels routine. The secretive assignment falls flat because it doesn't feel freeing. Most of us like to see big results when we spend precious moments working on a skill. Kids are the same way. That's where you and your child's teacher support get to shine. Go back to your pre-teen years. Do you remember any special, routine, joyful study session? You can easily think of two or three. That was the first sign that you left childhood and crossed the threshold into adult ways of thinking. Your child will also perform an adult-like task joyfully, even if it is against their will at times.

After all, you just finished an extraordinarily long day at work, sports, art, music, or dance class. Did the child return from the enrichment class exhausted, starving, or grumpy? Or full of energy? What happens when you don't feel your best? Then, the 8 or 9 PM hour doesn't look so inviting. You don't particularly care to spend an hour or more wrestling with any assignment, especially if the effort is not meaningful to you or the child.

Has this ever happened to you? Your child comes home without any homework. Hooray! But wait. Then the "I'm bored" monster appears. It's as though you - the parent - were also issued a secret assignment. What is the secret assignment? To make math workbook pages and closed reading assignments appear. Where does all this invisible homework come from? Suddenly, it has become your job to set up meaningful learning opportunities. Who has the time? Who has the energy?

CHAPTER 9

Assisting with Homework Assignments

The parents are encouraged to participate during the child's task performance process (mostly grades 1-8). The theoretical value of parental involvement in a child's schoolwork and homework has brought interest to educators, as it pertains to pedagogy reformation in the first decade of the 21st century. A couple of years ago, factors of parental involvement (talking and helping with homework) and students' academic achievements were being researched. The research conducted in 2014 found a clear link between students' achievements and their parents' help with math and reading. When giving elementary school students math problems to work on, parents chose different ways for them to complete the problems, according to Loyd Lanning: the parents were trying to reassure the children, make it possible for them to work without additional support, and also teach them to find a solution themselves.

The key to assisting with homework assignments is organization, and that hardly requires any advanced preparation. A good trick is to make a square table with 3 columns, with the first row having fewer lines than the second and the third. Then fill in the rows with possible stages of assignment completion. When the homework is given, lower the table so that the first line is visible, and so on. As the child completes each stage, emphasize it with two parallel lines. If the child is reading the keys from a printed piece of paper, for example, have the child strike through the completed stage. This time-tested system is very adaptable and useful when chores, grocery lists, and other similar tasks are scheduled. When choosing how your child will be spending this time, try to balance the complexity and number of possible stages with the child's age and abilities. Additionally, a system that works for one child might not suit the other, so it is important to be open to changes.

CHAPTER 10

Addressing Challenges and Frustrations

All the mom can do is hug Jack and tell him they will get through it. "It is difficult and we will talk about what happened after dinner, but right now I am really proud of the effort you are both making." During these moments Jack easily fills any uncomfortable silence with talk about rounding to the nearest whole number. It is obvious he is doing his best to work through the frustration. Dad usually reserves his interventions to when collective frustration is about to create a cloud of swearing. He has then removed them from the room individually to discuss the vocabulary they use to express themselves when they are frustrated. He reminds them that they are impeccable young people who have other words to call a math problem rather than). After these interruptions and distractions, Jack and his younger sister usually return to their work in an okay state of mind.

Encouraging older children to help their younger siblings with their homework can increase the misery index in a household. The older child reports that explaining how to round to the nearest whole number is driving both the seeker and the explainer to tears. A gentle reminder that it is important to learn to help each other even when it is hard fails to go over big with the red-eyed older child. "We needed more help than Jack," stated his sister before leaving the room. "This is ridiculous!"

CHAPTER 11

Promoting Independence and Responsibility

Set up a routine that works for everyone involved in the education of your child. Include responsibility during the weekend for some chores in the home. House chores help in nurturing the moral culture of a child. It might be befitting to sit down with your kids and break down this responsibility. They need to learn how to do them all. Not all will be done to perfection, but with time they will get used to and perfect the routine. Homework is compulsory, and allow them to understand that failure to adhere to home set routines will attract certain consequences. The consequences should be administered by the parent or guardian who is responsible for education in their daily life. Allowance need not be issued unless homework and house chores are properly done. If they are expected to eat, they should be expected not to fail.

Keep your child's books or research materials in an area where your child can access them. Support your child in selecting suitable workspaces, study spots, and seating that allow them comfort and independence to work. Ensure that the working space is equipped with ample space to store work materials. This space should be very close to a power point. Early years kids need to understand responsibility and being mindful of space. Have consequences if the above are violated. There should be a comfortable seating arrangement which allows for everything that is needed during a study session. This is inclusive of research materials and written work. Space should be available for spelling and wide spelling tests as well.

CHAPTER 12

Utilizing Technology as a Learning Tool

As the child advances in maturity and is able to conduct research on the Internet for informal tasks beyond the K-12 level, discuss the dangers online with them concerning privacy, decency, and adult supervision. There is much to learn about the internet, but the best of what the world has to offer is available to our children: learning to use it safely and effectively. In terms of the cognitive level and the academic field, the student requires an increased intellectual demand for the delivery of virtual classes at home. Reach out to your child's teacher if they are unable to execute the activity and rely on district-provided home learning.

Homework Assignments: Use good-quality educational websites to deepen your child's understanding of content they have learned in school. Encyclopaedia Britannica, Worldbook, and HowStuffWorks are good for general information. The Massachusetts Institute of Technology has the most famous of a number of free large-course offerings, but he or she can also attend free classes from Harvard, Duke, Caltech, and many other reputable institutions. Carefully follow the learning path of a website and your child's educational progress. This allows him or her to increase their independence as they master the requirements of a school grade. You can also give them additional work at the grade or content level at which they would like to move forward. Use online materials that include feedback or annotation to reinforce the quality of your child's independent work without a teacher.

CHAPTER 13

Balancing Homework with Other Activities

For school-age children, avoid signing them up for too many activities, instead prioritize family time. Being around parents or siblings is time well-spent for the kids' development. Family meals are well-proven together time, and the magical balance of fun-directing and reverting questions about schoolwork. Regular bed routine together, a good chat and a good book (checked with the teacher first for severity), will provide fond lasting memories for the kids along with good learning opportunities. Having at least a couple of (long) summer weeks without planned activities is also a guaranteed gain. Whatever you have read in the popular press, vacation beaches and playgrounds are important learning arenas for all children, especially for the youngest.

If there is a large discrepancy between the expectations of your child's new teacher and the daily homework routine in the previous school, just let it go (unless your child's teacher is open for a discussion). Teachers make the homework assignments, and they will be able to see how much time is needed to complete everything. See it as a collaboration between you and the teacher, making the best-informed plan for the child. Over time, resolve disparities gently by asking open-ended questions: How did you do today, what did you have to do, and how did you manage? It is important that the child grows into doing his or her own schoolwork, not that the homework stays the same amount of time.

CHAPTER 14

Communicating with Teachers and School Staff

Please keep in mind that typically teachers are not only managing their workload but also the online work of several students at once. The district offers the Google Classroom system, and while it is not our responsibility to manage that, teachers need platforms to effectively communicate with students and access ancillary material, including live lesson links. If you have any questions or concerns, it will likely be much more seamless to communicate with the appropriate school personnel than it would have been with your home-based team. If you are ever hard-pressed for any particular reason, you may always leave a message with Dr. Walker at (814)-825-4313 extension 4843. She will do her best to pass along the information promptly and appropriately.

If you would like to leave messages for your child's teachers and related service staff, please feel free to e-mail them. The e-mail prefix is always lowercase [first initial][last name]@flsd.net (or for a secretarial assistant, [last name]@flsd.net). If you would like for your child to keep a note somewhere, please let me know, and I will help to ensure the note is safe and brought to the teacher's attention. Teachers may also be reached through the ClassDojo; however, that is not the best method of communication on the Level 3/Phase 2 schedule, as everyone is working during those hours.

CHAPTER 15

Recognizing and Celebrating Achievements

If your child memorizes a sequence of numbers, for example, you might say, "Great memory work! I think you're ready for the next step, which is to also understand the meaning behind these numbers. Little steps like this add up to a lot of learning with many reasons to celebrate. Help your child see how most of their leaping comes from small jumps. This way, they won't rush through the small hurdles, excited for distant celebrations, but learn to feel each achievement every step of the way. They will be driven and motivated by their progress and will begin to strategically plan how to improve everyday. Then, in time, each of your child's little milestones should be reasons to party – with hats, horns, and cake. A little cake. Because they will need all the cake episodes to look forward to!

As the only adult in your child's academic world at home, it's important to recognize and celebrate their learning efforts. Don't think of celebration in the restricted sense of a party. This can be as simple as spotting a gradual increase in motivation and then congratulating your child on it. When we are happy or proud about what we are doing, the feeling motivates us to do even better. Children who find a sense of purpose and progress in their efforts are more likely to keep putting that effort to excel. Such children are also more likely to continue to acquire new skills and knowledge with little help from others.

CHAPTER 16

Supporting Emotional Well-being

It's important to help your child differentiate between the things they can and cannot control. They cannot control when the pandemic might be over or what measures they hear about others taking. What they can do instead is focus on the things they can control – such as sticking to a daily schedule, washing their hands, and other healthy behaviors. They can also exercise control over what they themselves can learn. Praise your child for the knowledge and skills they gain daily, and show them that you respect and value their effort. For instance, if your child is taking care of their younger siblings, that is something for you to value because they are helping the community stay strong and able to provide support and care for all its members. Encourage them to care for and make time for themselves before and after their school work. They can use part of their time to read for pleasure, play an instrument, watch TV, go for a walk with you, organize games, and other activities.

The Covid-19 pandemic has had a huge social and economic impact, and it's normal if your child is feeling frightened, lonely, or upset about the situation. You may want to give them your full attention during this time, but you may also be worried or stressed yourself. It is equally important to give yourself the time and space to manage your own feelings. It could be necessary to explain to your child the reason you need to step away for a while - if this is the case, be honest about this and let them know when you will be available to listen later. With young people not being able to leave their home and spend time with friends, their relationships with you will play an even greater role in their overall well-being.

CHAPTER 17

Encouraging Critical Thinking and Problem-Solving

Students are often taught an array of rote problem-solving techniques, even in mathematical disciplines. But without vigorous testing, these isolated ideas will not be at all connected to an understanding of interconnected mathematical principles. Try posing questions like "how does this technique differ from what we've learned?" Rather than just using rote memorization, students often develop creative methods to solve problems, provided with a number of alternatives, and having had detailed feedback from teachers and parents. During problem-solving, creative thinking is really needed. Students may think about a problem "in a brand new direction", leading to an improved learning model of key concepts.

Be creative in your learning "games". You could also generate a list of similar math problems in advance. To encourage students to think creatively about solutions, it can also be nice not to be at all interested in the final answer. By having your child explain a worked-out solution, you can also identify student misunderstandings. They may have worked out a highly convoluted scheme which you can help them to bypass in the future.

Encouraging critical thinking and problem-solving today, students are often memorizing how to solve math problems without understanding the principles. For example, you could provide your child with an estimate of a 3-digit number problem, like the number of seconds in one hour or weeks in a year. They can then compare it with the calculated exact answer to make sure that it at least reasonably makes sense. When they get older, practice breaking down complex problems into more manageable components. This often helps mentor them in the workplace in the future.

CHAPTER 18

Providing Resources for Additional Help

Peers: As always, other students can be a great resource. Groups of students often meet to assist one another with problem areas, review for exams, and offer moral support. You can also introduce your child to your peers who are good in a particular subject.

Internet: For help in a specific topic, you can check out the web. Many children's websites include educational areas, lesson plans for struggles in different subjects, online calculators, and more for particular homework assistance. For example, if your child is having trouble with the metric system, you can search for "metric system help" and may find an informative website that can aid in their understanding.

Kumon: These centers are found across the world, offering math and reading support at the student's pace and level. You can send your child there regularly or just for occasional support in specific areas of trouble.

Check the library: Most libraries now include nontraditional resources like reference sites and testing support. Many offer tutoring or study rooms, informational programming on a regular basis, links for homework support, as well as librarian support to direct you in your findings.

Here are a few options if your child needs help with a particular homework assignment or is struggling with an area of study:

CHAPTER 19

Monitoring Progress and Tracking Improvement

A household will evidence the principle of aiming to perfect a concept when a supportive member uses multiplicative rather than additive words to help a child surmount tiny mistakes (as attempted here) or solve arising issues. Many mistakes and much work call for "care", perchance with the occasional "concentrate"; in command of the correct concept, a consistently applied "brilliant!" will reassure and inspire with progress. Thoughts and ideas grow inside showing one's own experience doing activities sketched from examples at home and shares learning experiences so children become aware that everyone's skills progress with time. Learning is a process that deserves to be evaluated and documented to cater with needed, appropriately designed experiences in the environment for the tools that are accessible.

To be reassured that your child is heading in the right direction, some form of monitoring progress and tracking improvement becomes essential. Formal evaluations or testing often provide clinical independence. Tests help identify what is within the child's grasp, setting the stage to incorporate it into everyday learning routines. Expectations about test results must be discussed, framing feedback so children interpret it as a consequence of effort, regardless of what those results turn out to be. It attributes success not to some "gift" from the genes they did not select, but to resilience, practice, and persistence demonstrating genetic strength. The emphasis is put on growth in all the children's experiences rather than the type of intelligence that "Society" tends to admire for. As steps that bear fruits in normal, everyday tasks, all assessments are implemented, but are especially effective in activities that require little concepts.

CHAPTER 20

Facilitating Peer Collaboration and Support

Surprisingly, under these conditions, the emergent peer collaboration model, while essential for participation, had a negative impact on learning in the tested environment, demonstrating once again that more is not always better (we already knew this from our work in sleep research, which is perhaps the safest and most practiced monovariate theory in Biology). Given advancement over summer in children's self-regulated strategies predicting success, School of One already had all the tools to correct for these externalities. Stored triads also provided evidence that under the right conditions peer collaboration could be "taught," broadening the potential applicability of these paradigms.

Induced by a sudden move to online learning during COVID-19, an unplanned research project started internally at Studio Princeton by gathering best practices around learning support and family engagement. To our surprise, the top of the chart was not "containment or quiet time," a goal starting to receive ample coverage in the media since our move to "home-aloning" the children. It was, in fact, an amazing ability for children to connect and support each other in learning, typically only witnessed in school environments under the guidance of the teachers. Children would somehow initiate and manage these interactions themselves when given free rein and, seemingly, little involvement by adults at home. This model, emergent peer coaching, has shown at least some impact within the summer school environment but had not been directly tested in home learning environments.

CHAPTER 21

Promoting a Growth Mindset

Why is this? Well, a growth mindset (as opposed to a fixed mindset) means that learners believe (or are encouraged to believe) that ability can change over time. A growth mindset motivates a person to engage, to learn, and to improve. An open mindset means that failure does not bring a loss of self-worth, especially since self-worth is not tied to displays of natural talent. Instead, failure (or any form of shortcoming) is an essential part of learning, and therefore is something that is only considered part of the path to attaining knowledge. By celebrating the process, rather than the result, learners positively affirm their commitment to the open mindset. When learners believe that they can learn (and are thus a "work in progress"), they have no need to prove themselves "all at once". Instead, they attempt new challenges with a sense of equanimity.

Nobel Laureate, Arno Penzias once wrote in a book about one of the young researchers in his lab. He describes an A or B divide between two groups. The A group heard Dr. Penzias say, "You are smart. Good job." The B group heard Dr. Penzias say, "That was good - I think it's worth another look." In his own words, "(Julie) was definitely in the 'B group'... it really doesn't matter whether the 'chosen ones' are actually smarter than the rest; if the expectation is expressed, they (Julie's peers) do better."

CHAPTER 22

Fostering a Love for Learning

My boys have been steeped in a culture household filled with books and ferocious readers. They have reveled in words, stories, and wonder from a very young age. And their love of reading has supported their school endeavors. However, as they grow, reading (at least for pleasure) has taken a back seat to other interests. As a current educational ally, I must accept this stage for what it is, avoid practices that take away from their interest in the subject, and be open to other ways they choose to learn. Though what is difficult for me is that I understand what the boys have yet to discover: the world that books offer us when we are older, the curriculum they could enrich in formal schooling (and be enriched by it). I try, especially, not to sound disappointed or condescending towards them when offering thoughts on connecting reading with their learning chores.

While many of us - as children or adults - did not experience school as a place of joy, learning itself is often another matter. A professor of mine in graduate school once said, "Let school interfere as little as possible with your learning." Learning includes and transcends formal schooling. We do it as children and adults. It happens in and out of formal education systems. People revel in learning through play, from books, and from others. Sometimes we get the satisfaction of seeing a spark or a passion ignited in someone for the first time. Other times, we find ourselves staring in awe at someone's mastery of a subject or skill. Even in these dark days of COVID-19 when many now have firsthand experience of teaching or learning at home, we often focus on what has been lost: time, learning opportunities, and financial security.

CHAPTER 23

Encouraging Effective Note-Taking

1. Stress: sow good seeds also. Organizing notes visually with instructions for linkages and contexts will enhance learning. While presenting information, (a) copy figures, draw characters and write key words as cues inviting deeper processing, (b) mind map relationships and content, and (c) transparently illustrate saving evidence for points made, explanations or examples that have been elaborated upon; these "graphically organized notes... should enable students to recognize the relationships between vocabulary concepts and facts". Indeed, teacher and child collaboration to scaffold recognizing connected relationships between graphs and notes can further enhance learning.

Devices such as PCs, tablets, and smartphones are common tools for taking notes, but the best process for capturing important points during instruction is often unclear to our young students. Students commonly open a word processing document to take notes, but too often these typed notes suggest a tendency to record verbatim what they hear or see, rather than engage in the cognitive activity of internalizing, interpreting, and digesting to succinctly capture essential information in a form conducive to later use in self-regulated study. Insufficiently elaborate and generatively (ELG) aspects of student note-taking may contribute to the inconclusive research findings assessing performance effects of digital note-taking versus handwriting notes.

CHAPTER 24

Teaching Organization and Time Management Skills

Many parents worry about "forgotten assignments" and help too much with time management, causing their students to "forget" even longer. Cultivate patience and expectations for your child's developing sense of responsibility. If your child forgets about, or does not know how to do, their math or science homework at home, do nothing. This is a very different situation than when a child forgets his raincoat at home on a rainy day or forgets his backpack. I can assure you that any teacher will call to inform you if your child forgets their backpack containing more than the day's work. Misplacing homework documents at home is different. The pain of a lower mark usually teaches the child to bring home correct materials the following day, the lost effort clearly visible in the forever-lower average. Such consequences guide a student in a strictly "business" decision manner, without thinking it is the parent who must make them remember.

Younger elementary students tend to thrive when they are given structure and a specific time and place for doing their schoolwork. As you know, play is their work. Your child's quiet, comfortable and alone time for reading—natural and nicely spaced throughout the day and evening—will bring the best reading results. Family reading time can include both silent reading on different topics, or reading aloud from exciting stories that make children eager to jump in and explore further or just read more. Providing quiet, organized space and time for self-exploration and quiet reading gives children a quiet and peaceful retreat, a place to generate their own non-directed ideas or non-competitive physical play, which encourages a love of books, learning, and discovery that lasts a lifetime. One mother called the hour between 5 and 6 each evening her family's "reading hour," where no television, computer, or video games were permitted. Her children knew that between those hours they could do anything they'd like, as long as they'd read.

CHAPTER 25

Addressing Procrastination and Time Wasting Habits

The first part of this is helping kids develop better study habits and time management skills. A great starting point can be helping them create a study plan. This could be something they do themselves at the start of every study session, based on what they need to do that day, or it could cover a week at a time and establish good habits in which they regularly take a break, review old topics, and keep themselves on a schedule to complete necessary tasks on time. More information on how to do this can be found in this week's challenge in the 'Increasing Productivity' chapter. Another method of increasing productivity can be through the use of the Pomodoro Technique. This involves a study session lasting for 25 minutes, and then a five-minute break. After four sessions, they can take a longer break, typically lasting 15-30 minutes. In the breaks, kids can quickly vacate their workspace for a quick snack or a stretch, both to ensure they return back to work feeling refreshed.

One of the biggest roadblocks to success in learning at home is procrastination. When tasks pile up, it's easy to fall into the trap of putting things off until looming deadlines make it necessary to act. It's also common to waste a lot of time when trying to study or tackle an assignment - having trouble focusing on it means it takes longer to complete. This can lead to kids feeling like they are working all day, which makes it hard to muster the enthusiasm necessary to actually tackle the tasks they need to complete. But there are ways to help kids move past their natural inclination to put off unpleasant tasks and work more efficiently. Then it's important to address the larger cause of procrastination so that in the long run it becomes a rare occurrence.

CHAPTER 26

Helping with Test Preparation and Exam Strategies

1. Use the materials the teachers give you: Help your child to follow the test instructions. Follow the rubric, guidelines, and/or syllabus precisely. Your child should start with this task and follow instructions absolutely. Imagine your child is a robot locked in a briefcase with only the guidelines given by the teacher. The teacher's instructions are what the robot can know about the whole task over a long time. Therefore, make sure your child uses the teacher's materials each time. Also, be able to check that he/she follows the teacher's instructions well. If possible, email the teacher to verify they share all of their homework on their website and/or by emails to students and families. All families should receive emails from teachers. If they need more supplies, they can also request additional supplies from the teacher if they run out of time. 2. Repeat what you hear. It helps. Make sure your child repeats material from other formats multiple times. Post-it notes, rewritten or legible copied work, writing into their journal/notes what they hear, reading out loud, recording themselves reading, testing and retesting themselves - these are just the tip! 3. Quiz

each other. Quiz each other. You can abide your time and provide endless support and practice. 4. Stay on-task. Help your child stay on-task. If your child can stay focused, even if it is not for very long, he/she is more easily able to alleviate some of the stress that can accompany the daunting test preparation process. It can be helpful to offer adult support with time trials and time goals they want to exceed in order to complete study tasks.

Most students feel like test preparation is 'ruining their lives'. Their normal routine is interrupted by special test preparation homework. They are not in control of their schedule or given an end date to their discomfort. Most students feel robustly that they 'know' the material and therefore find it very hard to motivate themselves to fix it, check it, review it. They often find these four revision strategies useful. Here are ideas for maximizing the impact of the homework component of test/exam preparation for your child. These tips reflect what helps most when parents get involved with homework which has test preparation goals. There may be differences between individual students.

How can I help? The typical student experience:

CHAPTER 27

Supporting Reading Comprehension and Writing Skills

Address queries that arise from the literature lesson: What is the main point of this selection? Why would the character favor this perspective or express this feeling? Can you predict the outcome of this passage? Test predictions such as: You suspected the author used so many long descriptive phrases to illustrate what? Which personal experience of a singer will reinforce this conclusion? Encourage your adolescent to question the author. Dispute throughout or at the end of the reading test - 15 minutes can suffice - about the major challenges facing a particular character or antagonist. Solicit excerpts from the text for its internal thoughts or reflections. For instance, "What surrounded Emily when she personified the reliable gravity of her land inspired this sentence? What vocabulary accompanies the thought of someone who perceives something deeper, broader, more inclusive about her world as only a few poets can?" Assist your child in writing the most acceptable response, including relevant details and explanations. Practice writing responses that adhere to every reader's concept and incorporate transitional words.

The onset of adolescence triggers the development of deeper, more abstract or hypothetical problem-solving. To assimilate this blossoming intellectual ability with academic expectations, parents and teachers should support the arguments of critical thinking and reading comprehension. Fostering the ability to construct grammatically correct sentences can forge admirable writers as well as resilient thinkers.

CHAPTER 28

Promoting Healthy Sleep Habits

Ensuring that children sleep a healthy amount can be difficult in today's fast-paced world, but there are a few things that parents can do to help their children get the sleep they need. One of the first things parents can do to promote healthy sleep is to establish a set bedtime and stick to it, even on weekends or other days when a child has no obligations. You should also set a calming, consistent bedtime routine which can include reading a book together, talking about the day, taking a warm bath, practicing deep breathing exercises, or going through a yoga and/or meditation sequence if it's not too stimulating for your child. Finally, parents can be mindful of sleep "helpers" and "deterrence" - blocking rock music, a black metal headboard, or hanging a quilt which has had its colors faded by the sun might sound bizarre, but such measures can have an impact on how a child sleeps.

Be mindful of sleep helpers and deterrence: On days when the whole family can sleep in a little longer, consider keeping the curtains open just a tad later than normal to help create a natural wake-up process for your child. Creating a nighttime environment that mimics nature's natural light and dark conditions is important to help promote healthy sleep habits, and the same is true for waking your child peacefully and calmly. On the other hand, be very mindful of using screens too late in the evening. The blue light from screens has been shown to disrupt sleep habits by negatively affecting melatonin production, and too much stimulating sensory information right before bed can also make it difficult to fall asleep.

Set a calming, consistent bedtime routine: Creating a calming bedtime routine for your child does not have to be an elaborate event, but it can be a special time for you to connect with your child that also helps prepare them for a good night's sleep. Try reading a book together, talking about the day, having your child take a warm bath, practicing deep breathing exercises, or going through a yoga or meditation sequence if those activities are not too stimulating for your child. The most important thing is to be consistent with your routine to help your child's body relax and prepare for sleep.

One of the first things you can do to promote healthy sleep is to establish a set bedtime and stick to it. Bedtimes may need to vary slightly by the child, but having a set bedtime can help the body regulate itself to fall asleep and wake up more naturally.

In the context of a school day, sleep researcher Dr. Jodi Mindell suggests that elementary school students should be getting about 10 hours of sleep each night, with high school students getting about 8 to 10 hours. Ensuring that children sleep a healthy amount can be difficult in today's fast-paced world, but there are a few things that parents can do to help their children get the sleep they need.

Promoting healthy sleep habits is an important part of raising children who are ready to meet their full potential. There are many theories about the role of sleep in learning, with some arguing that sleep is time for the brain to recharge and others suggesting that it is a time when the brain solidifies the new knowledge gained throughout the day. Regardless of which theory you subscribe to, most adults agree that sleep is essential for the amount of learning our children are doing.

CHAPTER 29

Encouraging Physical Activity and Breaks

When children engage in learning, it is essential to offer multiple breaks. Children need small "rewards" or motivation acts to continue being focused and involved in assignments given by parents, and to continue learning as best as they can. Use short breaks between school subjects or activities. You can be flexible and offer breaks as needed. Our youngest participants, aged 8, recommended 10 to 20 minutes of breaks not including any homework time. Assignments should also not exceed 30 minutes for our oldest participants aged 17. Breaks are beneficial when communication and parent-child attachment are strengthened. Lastly, breaks allow constant physical movement, which helps cognition through learning and brain development. Enhance and extend learning with the help of technology. Many websites and apps are offering temporary free access and new content free previews. Use these resources to enhance learning content. Online games, documentaries, virtual museum visits, and virtual interactive toolkits can be used to generate interest in specific areas of learning. For example, you can extend learning by incorporating cooking activities when covering math (e.g., measuring) and science topics (e.g., digestion or physical changes).

Encourage physical activity and breaks from learning. When possible, children should get at least one hour of physical activity per day.

Physical activity is beneficial for children's mental and physical well-being, and can help lessen feelings of anxiety and loneliness. Physical activity is also an essential part of learning, since it enhances children's cognitive skills, including their concentration, attention, and memory. Physical activity is beneficial for learning a second or additional language since it involves different cognitive skills depending on the activity, like memory, multitasking, creativity, and attention. You can encourage your children to be active by being active with them, using preferred activities, and including movement into learning activities. Plan physical activities your family enjoys for when school subjects are covered, make sure children engage in moderate to vigorous physical activity with large muscle groups every day.

CHAPTER 30

Nurturing Creativity and Critical Thinking

I am honored to have a chance to help guide a bit in the ways of thinking and creating. I am humbled by the challenge. You are traversing new lands each day and each moment is a chance for truly awe-inspiring change. Your apparently infinite blueprints for the universe are sparking off of each other, and from within an entirely internal process, new art or innovation arises. Your thoughts are nowhere but inside your mind, until they are fully formed. For so long they are nothing that others can hold or examine, until they are put into a medium that other people can appreciate with all of their senses, or even take up and manipulate themselves. Your art or innovation then is something that somehow transcends your own head – itself a mystery of mysteries – into something that is universal, though new.

My favorite thing is to watch your mind in action. I love to see the wheels turning. I love to overhear your thoughts. I love to find the ideas and connections you've scribbled down in your notebooks. And most of all, I love to watch you manipulate colors or words or notes or food to make those thoughts come into the world in ways others can also appreciate. Watching your thinking evolve is like watching the fractal images you love to draw: an infinitely complex but clear and beautiful process that is always utterly unique and surprisingly similar each time I view a new vignette.

CHAPTER 31

Balancing Screen Time and Homework

So if I ask my child to limit screen time to an hour once they come home from school, is a weekend game of Fortnite at a friend's house also counted? I still recommend that Screen Time across the entire week remain meaningful and educational. Yet something else happens here. The explicit encouragement of going over to a friend's to play the physical game of Uno or Scrabble or to play a board game for away from home screentime takes form, a feature we may have forgotten as we had explicitly discouraged phone calls apart from conducting homework. Here at last can help out our intent to create more Face Time.

The next paragraph is a list of educational sites which came from the school's list (Edutopia, for example, ReadWorks, for example, or Illinois Digital Archives for Social Studies and Science topics, for example). We do not just try to avoid our kids' hands-on time on the internet going toward video games, for example, but also have our child try to avoid having the screen play a passive role. I admit, as a teacher, I even tweak this by having my child download books onto my phone to be read on a car trip for a dramatic drop of Screen Time because the screen becomes an electronic book, no longer just being a screen.

Screentime includes anything on the internet. This question is often asked, but there is no optimal time. The classic guideline for screen time and children is the American Association for Pediatrics, which limits screen time for over six-year-olds to one hour. But screen time is not just about quantity, but it is also about what the screen is doing. We do not simply ask our child to go to the internet to look up answers by having our child go to educational sites as much as possible for educational screen time.

CHAPTER 32

Conclusion

In the 1970s, when my father and I still lived in Italy, I had to let myself into our town's public library every day around 5 each day after school. While my dad worked there supervising the study hall and doing his own writing, I had to decide how to spend my time. In an earlier period of European history read to me from a collection of History of War magazines. Later I spent my time painting, reading murder mysteries or learning English vocabulary with a stack of dragged-out-of-the-closet LearnInOne-Minute-A-Day English language books that argued that fluency would be mine by my next trip to the barber. All in all, it was a bolt-hole, and I have no doubt that the formless time spent pursuing odd passions was a major influence on my eventual career.

The reality, for many parents, is that all their good intentions quickly unravel in the face of the daily necessity of wading through homework with their children. So even if homework hasn't had a significant effect on children's achievement so far, many parents may still buy into the idea that they will in the future. My own suggestion is that homework policies should prescribe amounts of homework, and even establish study nights once per week where families can join together as others and work on their students' homework, as a way to ensure that family time is rigorously protected. The school schedule, and ordinary family life, leave us with very few opportunities to really make the time we are together matter. Providing help, in person, for homework is a way to assure that the pressure on parents to click a button and keep moving through the daily routine of homework can be relaxed.